Animal Neighbours
Mole

Stephen Savage

Sch

Animal Neighbours

Titles in this series:

Badger • Bat • Deer • Fox • Hare • Hedgehog
Mole • Mouse • Otter • Owl • Rat • Swallow

Conceived and produced for Hodder Wayland by

Nutshell
MEDIA

Intergen House, 65–67 Western Road, Hove BN3 2JQ, UK
www.nutshellmedialtd.co.uk

Commissioning Editor: Vicky Brooker
Designer: Tim Mayer
Illustrator: Jackie Harland
Picture Research: Glass Onion Pictures

Published in Great Britain in 2004 by Hodder Wayland, an imprint of Hodder Children's Books.

This paperback edition published in 2007 by Wayland, an imprint of Hachette Children's Books.

British Library Cataloguing in Publication Data
Savage, Stephen, 1965–
Mole. – (Animal neighbours)
1. Moles (Animals)– Juvenile literature
I. Title
599.3'35

ISBN-13: 978 0 7502 5080 1

Cover: A mole looking out from a molehill.
Title page: A mole looking for food above ground.

Picture acknowledgements
FLPA 10, 19, 20, 21, 23, 28r, 28l (V. Giannotti); Natural Science Photos 24 (Steve Downer), 25 (Ray Kennedy); naturepl.com 12–13 (Geoff Dore), 26–27 (Duncan McEwan); NHPA *Cover* (Manfred Danegger), 11 (Laurie Campbell), 13t (Michael Leach); OSF *Title page* (Hans Reinhard), 6 (Donald Secker), 8, 9, 16 (OSF), 17 (Hans Reinhard), 22 (Robin Redfern), 27t, 28t (OSF), 28b (Hans Reinhard); Still Pictures 7 (Roland Seitre).

Colour reproductions by Dot Gradations Ltd, UK
Printed and bound in China.

Wayland,
an imprint of Hachette Children's Books
338 Euston Road, London NW1 3BH

Contents

Meet the Mole

The mole is a small, active mammal that lives in underground tunnels. It burrows beneath open fields, woodlands, gardens and parks, and can be found across Europe, Asia and North America.

This book is about the European mole, a common species that lives in Europe and Asia.

▲ **The red shading on this map shows where European moles live in the world today.**

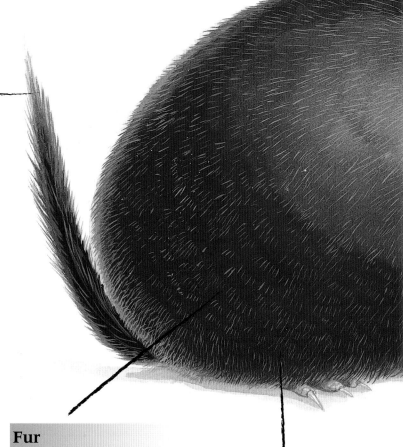

Tail

Moles have sensory hairs on their tails, which help to detect prey and to find their way around.

MOLE FACTS

The European mole's scientific name is *Talpa europaea*. This comes from the Latin words *talpa* meaning 'mole' and *europaea* meaning 'Europe'.

Other common names include 'common mole', 'earthmover', 'dirt eater' and 'blind dog'.

Males are known as boars, females as sows and young moles as pups.

Adult males can be 12–17 cm long and weigh 87–120 g. Females are 11–14 cm long and weigh 72–106 g.

Fur

The mole's short, velvety fur is waterproof.

Hind legs

The mole's hind legs are smaller than the front legs. They are used to brace the mole's body against the tunnel walls, giving the front legs extra leverage.

4

▲ **This shows the size of a European mole compared to an adult human hand.**

Ears

Moles have poor hearing. They have no external ear flaps, but the ear channel can be closed when digging to keep out any soil.

Eyes

Moles have very small eyes that are often buried in the fur. They have poor eyesight, but their eyes are sensitive to changes in light and dark.

Snout

The mole has a good sense of smell. The fleshy nose pad is covered in thousands of sensory hairs, which are similar to those on its tail.

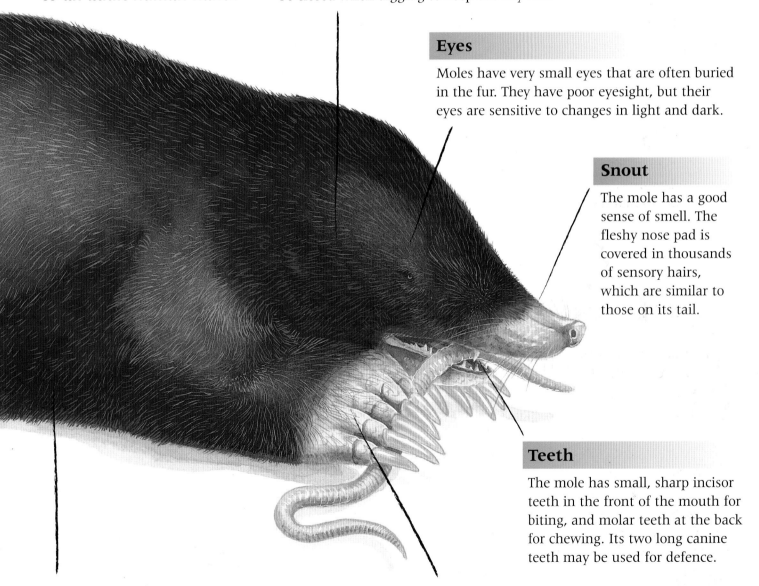

Teeth

The mole has small, sharp incisor teeth in the front of the mouth for biting, and molar teeth at the back for chewing. Its two long canine teeth may be used for defence.

Skin

The mole's skin is more sensitive to touch than any other mammal's, which probably helps it find its way around the dark tunnels.

Front legs

The mole's muscular, spade-like front legs end with large claws, which are excellent for digging.

5

The Mole Family

The European mole belongs to the mole family, a group that contains 29 species of moles and desmans. All moles are expert diggers and live underground. While most live mainly in their underground tunnels, a few species, such as the least shrew mole, are active above ground as well.

All moles are carnivores and have a large appetite, which is necessary to give them the energy they need for digging. The Townsend mole is one of the few species that also eats root crops and plant leaves.

▼ The snout of the star-nosed mole has 22 sensitive tentacles on the end. These are used for finding food in soil or water.

BIGGEST AND SMALLEST

The biggest member of the mole family is the Russian desman, from south-east Europe and central Asia. This mole can grow up to 22.9 cm long, excluding the tail.

The smallest mole is the shrew mole from North America, which is just 7.6 cm long.

▲ The Russian desman has thick fur to protect it from the cold weather and water.

Desmans are specially adapted to a semi-aquatic life. They live near water and eat aquatic invertebrates and small fish, which they catch underwater. Desmans have webbed feet and a scaly, flattened tail. Their long, flexible snout reaches food at the bottoms of lakes, streams and ponds. Desmans build nests but they rarely dig tunnels.

Birth and Growing Up

It is springtime, and a pregnant female mole prepares to give birth. She digs a special chamber at the end of a short tunnel, where she lines a nest with dried leaves and grass. When the nest is complete, the sow gives birth to a litter of pups. These tiny moles are born with no fur and with their eyes tightly closed.

The sow does not stay with her pups for long. She leaves them curled up in the safety of the nest while she travels through the rest of her tunnels to find food. The sow returns to the nest every four to six hours to suckle her pups.

◀ New-born mole pups are blind, deaf and unaware of their surroundings.

8

MOLE PUPS

New-born mole pups weigh about 3.5 g. By the time they are 3 weeks old they weigh 40 g. By 3 months old they weigh the same as an adult mole.

A sow normally gives birth to a litter of four pups, although it can be as few as two or as high as seven. She produces just one litter a year.

▲ These young mole pups have just started to grow their black, velvety fur.

When they are 2 weeks old, the mole pups start to grow fur. By the time they are 3 weeks old their eyes are open, but like their parents, their eyesight is very poor. They can crawl about but will stay in the nest chamber.

Early days

The sow continues to return to the nest to suckle her pups until they are just over 4 weeks old. By this time the pups have become much more active and start to leave the nest chamber. They begin to eat solid food, such as insects and worms, which they find in the tunnels. When they are 5 weeks old, the pups are fully weaned and eating only solid food.

▲ This young mole has caught a worm that it found dangling through the tunnel ceiling.

Soon after they are weaned, the young moles are driven out of their mother's tunnels. Now they must find their own territory in which to dig new tunnels.

This is a time of great danger for young moles because they must travel overground, where predators such as owls, kestrels, foxes and cats might see them. If they are lucky, they may find an old, disused mole tunnel, which will save them the work of digging a new one.

DANGEROUS TIMES

Young moles may travel up to 1 kilometre above ground before they find a place to burrow. Many pups choose unsuitable sites to dig their tunnels. If they dig them in soil that has poor drainage, or that is close to water, the moles can drown when the tunnels become flooded in heavy rain.

▼ This fox can smell a mole burrowing underground and is frantically trying to dig it up.

Habitat

Moles live wherever the soil is deep enough for tunnelling, and where there is enough prey. Their favourite habitats are grassland and farmland, where they can build a large network of tunnels in the deep soil. Other habitats include the edges of deciduous woodland, hedgerows, and even light forest, where the trees are far apart. The soil in thicker forests is too thin for moles to burrow. Moles also enter gardens and parks that are near or in the countryside.

SCENT-MARKING

Once they have found their own territory and started burrowing, young moles deposit scent around their tunnels from scent glands on their bodies. The scents let other moles know that the territory is already taken.

▼ Large numbers of molehills often appear in the spring, when moles are extending their feeding tunnels or boars are looking for sows.

Moles avoid areas that are permanently wet, where their tunnels may be at risk of flooding. They also avoid soils that are too stony, or that are too sandy or acidic, such as sand dunes and moorland. These soils are not compact enough for digging tunnels, and do not contain as much food.

◀ Moles like gardens with big lawns, where they can dig a large network of tunnels.

Tunnel system

Male and female moles live alone, each having their own separate, ever-expanding tunnel system. This will contain several tunnels, most of which are used for feeding. The sides of the feeding tunnels are rubbed smooth by the mole's constant movement through them. Ventilation tunnels run vertically to the surface to let in fresh air.

Some tunnels are permanent, while others are only temporary. Temporary tunnels are built in shallow soil, or where there are sudden concentrations of worms near the surface, such as in newly ploughed fields.

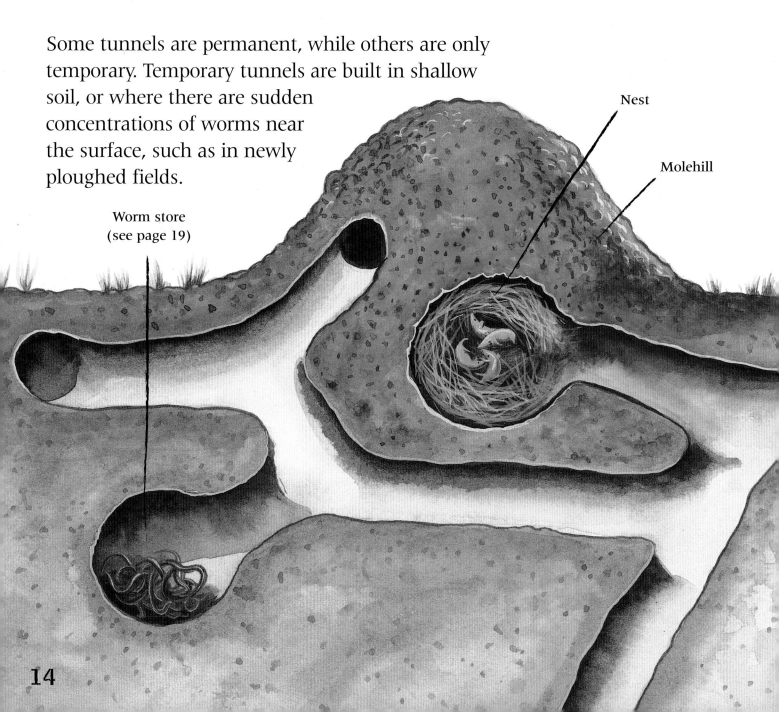

Nest

Molehill

Worm store
(see page 19)

MOLEHILLS

Molehills are created by the soil that is pushed out by a mole as it digs a tunnel. To dig a tunnel, the mole pushes its hind legs against the tunnel wall while it scoops out soil using its fore legs. The mole then turns round and pushes the loose soil along a side tunnel leading to the surface, and out above ground to form a molehill.

▼ The mole's tunnel system is a home, a place to rear young and a means of catching food.

Permanent tunnels are dug at different depths in the soil, from 30–70 centimetres. The deepest tunnels are used in times of drought. This is when worms move deeper underground in search of wetter soil, to prevent their bodies from drying out. The deeper tunnels are also used in the winter, when it is cold above ground and in the upper levels of soil.

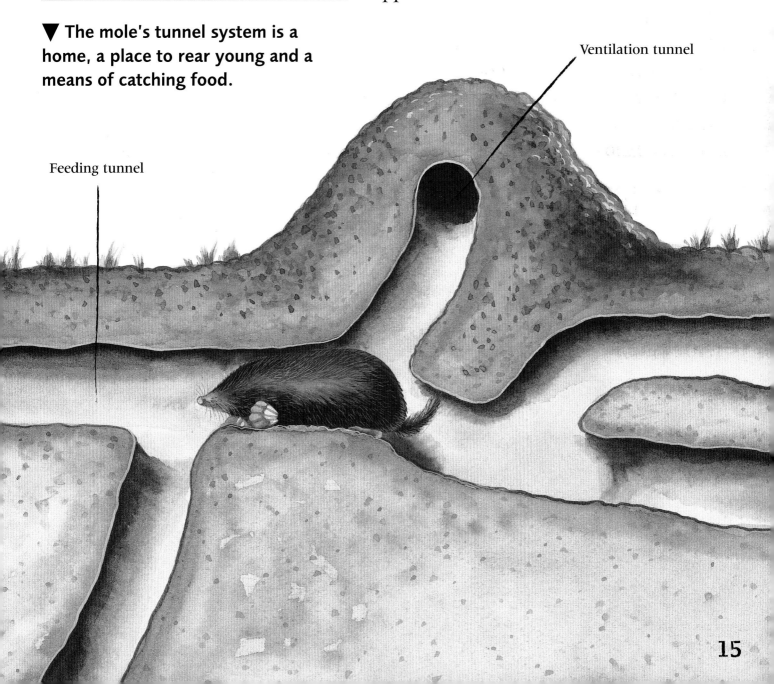

Ventilation tunnel

Feeding tunnel

▲ Young mole pups are protected from predators and the weather in nests deep within the tunnel system.

The nest

A mole's tunnel system may contain several nests. One will be used for raising young, while the others are used for sleeping or resting. The nests are built in small chambers, which are lined with dry leaves and grass to form a rough ball shape.

To collect the nest materials, moles must venture above ground. If they are lucky, they will find the materials close to the tunnel entrance and drag them into the burrow. If they have to travel further from the entrance, they risk being attacked by predators.

▼ Moles will only travel above ground when there is no other choice.

Fortresses

Moles sometimes build an extra-large molehill known as a fortress. This can be 0.5 metres high and 2 metres in diameter. Unlike most molehills, fortresses are so big that they contain one or more nests and a network of tunnels. The mound will also have one or more food stores. A fortress is usually built in areas with shallow soil where moles cannot dig very deep. They may also be built in areas prone to flooding, where they can be a refuge from the water.

Food and Hunting

Moles are insectivores that feed on a variety of invertebrates. Their most important prey are earthworms. They also eat many different insects, insect larvae and slugs, which also live underground. Insects make up most of the mole's diet in the hot summer months, when earthworms are harder to find. In winter, when most insects are hibernating or surviving as eggs waiting for the spring, earthworms are the mole's main prey.

▼ Moles eat lots of small animals, but they also have many larger predators. (The illustrations are not to scale.)

Mole food chain

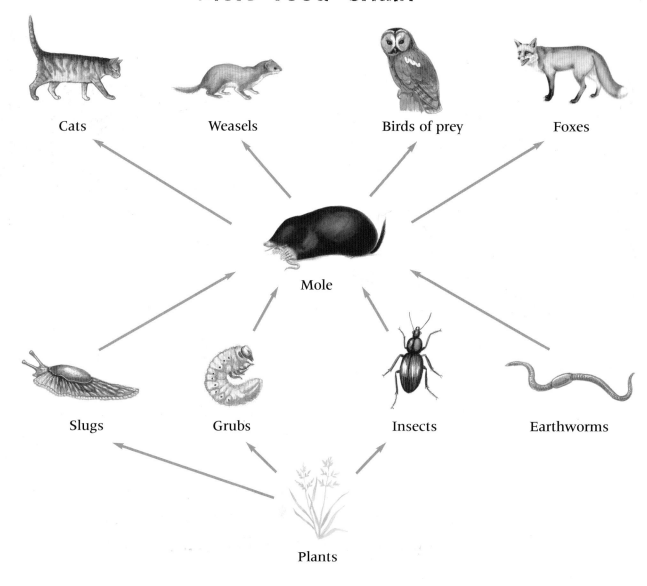

Cats

Weasels

Birds of prey

Foxes

Mole

Slugs

Grubs

Insects

Earthworms

Plants

WORM STORE

When lots of worms fall into a mole's tunnels, there can be too many to eat all at once, so the mole will collect them and store them in special chambers. To stop the worms escaping, the mole bites their head segment. This disables the worms but does not kill them, so they stay alive and fresh for eating later.

▲ A mole uses its large front legs to pin down a struggling earthworm.

There are several types of earthworm, all of which provide moles with a good-sized meal. This is important because moles must eat more than half their body weight in food a day. Earthworms are also a good source of moisture because their bodies are made up of 85 per cent water. This means a mole regularly eating earthworms can survive without actually drinking. One hectare of grassland may contain as many as 6 million earthworms.

Hunting

Moles catch most of their food from the floor of their underground tunnels. Many worms and insect larvae burrow into the soil. When they break through the roof of a mole's tunnel, they fall through on to the floor and become easy prey. Moles spend most of their waking hours travelling through their tunnel systems hunting for such prey. They are active both day and night, spending about four hours hunting followed by about four hours of rest.

▼ A slug's slimy body will stop many animals from eating it, but this does not put off the mole.

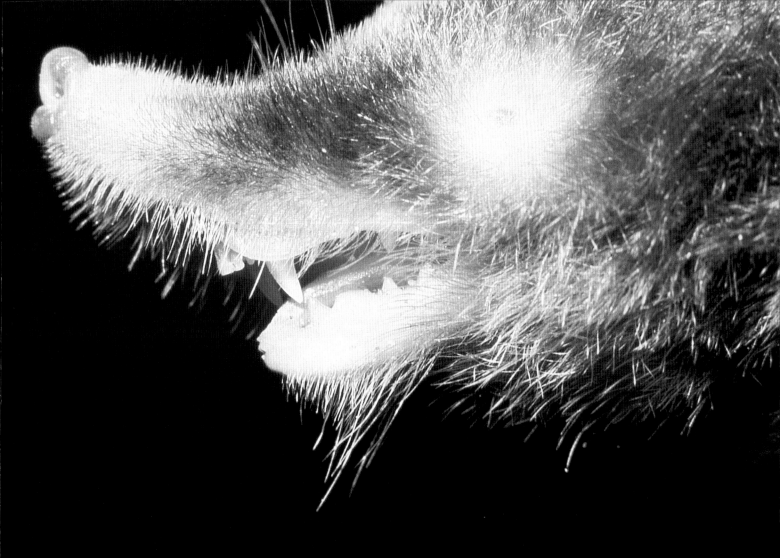

▲ **This close-up photograph of a mole's snout shows its sensitive hairs and sharp, pointed teeth.**

In the summer, during long periods of very hot weather, earthworms may burrow too deep in the soil for moles to find. If no food enters the burrow, the mole will leave its tunnels and hunt insects above ground. Moles hunt outside their tunnels during the night, when it is cooler and there are more insects around. Without earthworms to provide water, a mole may also need to find water above ground or die from dehydration.

HAIR SENSE

Moles detect their prey using the thousands of tiny sensitive hairs on their snouts. The snout is very mobile, like an elephant's trunk, and the hairs can detect the slightest movement of an insect, worm or slug in the tunnel.

Finding a Mate

By the time they are 10 months old, both male and female moles are fully grown and ready to mate. In March, at the start of the breeding season, boars start tunnelling over a larger area in search of sows.

When a boar breaks through the tunnel of another mole, he will check for scent marks to find out if it belongs to a boar or a sow. If the tunnel belongs to a boar, the invading male will retreat. If it belongs to a sow, he will seek her out and they will mate.

▼ **This male mole is approaching another mole's nest with caution, ready to defend itself with its front claws if it is attacked.**

FIGHTING

Apart from in the breeding season, between March and May, moles avoid each other whenever possible. Even male and female moles keep apart outside the breeding season, since both are equally as aggressive. If two moles do meet they will fight, sometimes to the death.

▲ **Moles will chase each other through the tunnels and fight until one mole retreats.**

There is no real bond between the male and female moles and a few hours after mating, the boar will leave the sow and not return. If the boar comes across another sow on his travels he will mate with her as well. The sow will be pregnant for 30 days after mating, before giving birth.

Threats

Moles can live for up to 6 years in the wild, but most moles will not live any longer than 3 years. Since moles spend most of their life underground they can avoid many predators. Their main underground threat comes from weasels, which can enter a mole's tunnels, catching and eating the adult and any young they may find in the nest.

When moles dig tunnels just below the surface of the ground, their movement can sometimes be spotted by a heron. This large bird can catch moles by stabbing its long, sharp beak into the ground.

▲ Weasels are aggressive predators that eat a variety of small mammals, including moles. This one has caught a wood mouse.

Moles that are forced to leave their tunnels and go above ground in search of food and water are very vulnerable to predators. At night the biggest danger comes from owls, which swoop down from the sky. Young moles live above ground for some time before establishing their own territory. Many are eaten by predators such as owls, buzzards, foxes, cats and dogs.

▼ Moles can swim if necessary. This one has been caught by a European otter, although such incidents are rare.

People and moles

People have always been the mole's greatest enemy. Many farmers and gardeners regard them as pests because of the damage their tunnelling can cause. Surface tunnels in farmland can disturb the roots of crops, causing them to wilt and die. Molehills and stones brought to the surface by their digging can damage farm machinery, and ruin garden lawns and sports greens.

▼ In the past, professional mole-catchers displayed the moles they caught as proof of their success.

At the beginning of the twentieth century, millions of moles were killed by professional mole-catchers. They sold the highly prized moleskins to be made into expensive clothes. These included fashionable waistcoats worn by men, and long coats, muffs and hats worn by women.

Today, most moles are killed using traps or poison. Yet despite the damage they cause, moles can also be beneficial to people. They prey on many harmful insect larvae that damage plants and crops, and their tunnels help drain and add air to the soil.

▲ The traditional scissor trap has been used to catch moles in their tunnels for over 100 years.

27

Mole Life Cycle

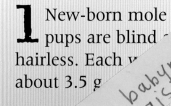

1 New-born mole pups are blind and hairless. Each weighs about 3.5 g.

The babymol is 10 l 535.91S thebaby

2 By the time they are 3 weeks old, the pups' eyes are open and they have started to grow fur.

5 Moles are mature at the age of 10 months and will be able to mate in the next breeding season.

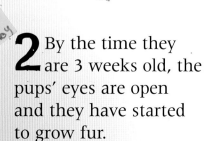

3 At just over 4 weeks old, the pups will leave the nest and start to eat solid food.

4 At 5 weeks, the pups will leave their mother's tunnels and travel overground, eventually building their own tunnel system.

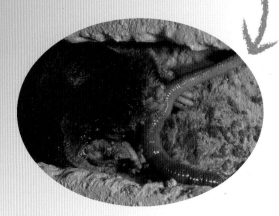

Mole Clues

Look out for the following clues to help you find signs of a mole:

Molehills
The best clues to the underground presence of moles are their molehills. These are small piles of fine, fresh earth up to 30 centimetres in diameter, particularly visible in fields.

Young moles
Young moles can be spotted living above ground as they look for somewhere to dig their first tunnel.

Fortresses
These are particularly large molehills, about 0.5 metres high and 2 metres in diameter. They are usually built for nesting in places where the soil is not good enough for tunnelling, or in places close to water, where underground tunnels would be at risk from flooding.

Surface tunnels
Sometimes it can be possible to see surface tunnels above the ground because the top of the tunnel is forced slightly above ground level.

Digging
Signs of movement at the top of a molehill may mean that a mole is pushing soil out of its tunnel below. Occasionally you may get a quick glimpse of the mole.

Birds
Look out for birds such as thrushes and blackbirds on molehills. They feed on insects and worms brought up with fresh soil, which means a mole may be tunnelling beneath.

Footprints
Moles rarely leave footprints above ground, but you may find them in a molehill. The front footprints are made by the claws, which are the only part of the foot to touch the ground.

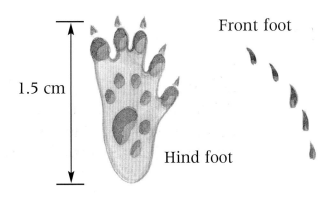

1.5 cm

Front foot

Hind foot

Glossary

boar A male mole. Male pigs, badgers and hedgehogs are also called boars.

canine teeth Sharp, extra-long teeth used for killing prey.

carnivores Animals that eat other animals.

deciduous Trees that lose their leaves in the autumn.

dehydration The loss of too much water from the body of an animal or plant.

drought When no rain falls for a long period of time and the soil at the surface becomes dry and hard.

habitat The area where an animal or plant naturally lives.

hibernating In a deep sleep that lasts most of the winter.

incisor teeth Front teeth for cutting and biting.

insectivore An animal that eats mainly insects.

invertebrates Animals that do not have a backbone.

larvae An early stage in the development of an insect.

litter A group of young animals that are born at the same time from the same mother.

predator An animal that kills and eats other animals.

prey Animals that are killed and eaten by predators.

pup A young mole. Young dogs, seals and rats are also called pups.

scent glands Glands that produce a special scent for marking territories.

semi-aquatic An animal or plant that lives on land and in water.

sow A female mole. Female pigs, badgers and hedgehogs are also called sows.

suckle When a mother allows her young to drink milk from her teats.

territory The area that is defended and controlled by an animal.

weaned A young mammal is weaned when it stops taking milk from its mother and eats only solid food.

Finding Out More

Other books to read

Animal Young: Mammals by Rod Theodorou (Heinemann, 2000)

Classification: Animal Kingdom by Kate Whyman (Wayland, 2000)

Classifying Living Things: Classifying Mammals by Andrew Solway (Heinemann, 2003)

From Egg to Adult: The Life Cycle of Mammals by Mike Unwin (Heinemann, 2003)

Illustrated Encyclopedia of Animals by Fran Pickering (Chrysalis, 2003)

Junior Nature Guides: Mammals (Chrysalis, 2003)

Life Cycles: Cats and Other Mammals by Sally Morgan (Chrysalis, 2003)

Living Nature: Mammals by Angela Royston (Chrysalis, 2004)

New Encyclopedia of Mammals by David Macdonald (OUP, 2001)

Reading About Mammals by Anna Claybourne (Watts, 2000)

The Wayland Book of Common British Mammals by Shirley Thompson (Wayland, 2000)

Weird Wildlife: Mammals by Jen Green (Raintree, 2003)

What's the Difference?: Mammals by Stephen Savage (Wayland, 2002)

Wild Britain: Parks & Gardens, Meadows by R. & L. Spilsbury (Heinemann, 2002)

Organisations to contact

Countryside Foundation for Education
PO Box 8, Hebden Bridge HX7 5YJ
www.countrysidefoundation.org.uk
An organisation that produces training and teaching materials to help people understand the countryside and its problems.

English Nature
Northminster House, Peterborough, Cambridgeshire PE1 1UA
www.english-nature.org.uk
A government body that promotes the conservation of English wildlife and the natural environment.

The Mammal Society
2B Inworth Street,
London SW11 3EP
www.abdn.ac.uk/mammal/
Promotes the study and conservation of British mammals.

Wildlife Watch
National Office, The Kiln, Waterside, Mather Road, Newark NG24 1WT
www.wildlifetrusts.org
The junior branch of the Wildlife Trusts, a network of local Wildlife Trusts caring for nature reserves, and protecting a huge number of habitats and species.

Index

Page numbers in **bold** refer to a photograph or illustration.